Cover image from Mrs. John Adams Conant by William Dunlap,
Metropolitan Museum of Art.
ISBN: 978-1546681632

Published by:
Michigan Writers Cooperative Press
P.O. Box 1505
Traverse City, Michigan 49685

AND SARAH
HIS WIFE

CHRISTINA
DIANE
CAMPBELL

MICHIGAN WRITERS
COOPERATIVE PRESS
2017

To everyone in basements everywhere...

There are eight rooms upon the first floor...with most delightful cellars under them. —Wilson Miles Gary, about Patrick Henry's mansion Scotchtown in Ashland, Virginia (*The Virginia Gazette*, April 1782)

The story told by respected biographers, Internet pundits, and Hanover County residents goes like this: In 1775, the great American orator Patrick Henry gave his famous "Give me liberty or give me death" speech before a divided Virginia legislature, persuading them to take arms against the British. He illustrated his speech by standing like a manacled prisoner, hands crossed over his chest so that chains were almost visible on his wrists. This happened just weeks after his wife Sarah "Sallie" Shelton Henry died, insane and locked in the basement of Patrick's plantation mansion, Scotchtown. During the last three years of her life, she was prone to violence, and for her own safety wore a long-sleeved "strait-dress" that crossed her arms over her chest.

The story is riveting, but is it true?

I first learned about the legend of Sarah Henry in a book about ghosts in Virginia. According to that account, she haunts the basement of Scotchtown, in Ashland, Virginia. The Association for the Preservation of Virginia Antiquities (APVA) maintains the plantation. Caretakers and former residents say they have heard Sarah's pained cries flying up from the cellar.

At the time I read the ghost book, I was recovering from severe mental illness myself. I'd had Obsessive Compulsive Disorder (OCD) for a few years, until a psychiatrist put me on the antidepressant Luvox. I was a lucky woman; it worked. My hundreds of constant, crazy ruminations—such as, "Did I hit a pothole or a person? Pothole or person?"—became occasional whispers. Although Sarah's and my illnesses were almost certainly different, I figured we both knew the agony of a brain gone lopsided. A bubble of empathy for Sarah sat in my heart for a couple years, until a writing professor in graduate school told us to research a historical figure, write a profile, and cite sources. As the professor explained the assignment, I became a bit unhinged with anticipation. I thought about touring Scotchtown. Maybe from the corner of my eye, I would see a wispy, white woman; only I would notice her, because we had an inter-dimensional understanding of the lonely pain of mental illness. I still suffered from the shock of learning that I was—had been?—mentally ill. I also still suffered from the shock of recovery, which was similar to the feeling of putting on new glasses. "Oh, so this is how the world should look!" creates the same intakes of breath as, "Oh, this is how my brain is supposed to work!" I still felt perched on the edge of existence, and with Sarah Henry I was looking for someone else who did as well.

The sun warmed my windshield as I drove the couple hours to Scotchtown from my home in Centreville, Virginia. I cranked down the driver's window and the opposite backseat window. This configuration created a cool current of air that circled against the back of my neck. I listened to Paul Simon's song "Born at the Right Time" because it seemed to fit. Here I was, newly happy, newly grounded, perhaps a bit pudgier than before the Luvox, and I was on my way to visit a woman born several centuries too early for such pharmaceuticals.

On the Scotchtown tour, I didn't see her. Of course I didn't. I didn't hear any thumps, or feel any drafts. In our group of about eight people, I was the only one who asked the docent about paranormal activity.

"I've never experienced anything, myself," said the docent. She didn't look at me.

"Has anyone else?" I said. I couldn't let go.

"I think someone said they saw a woman in colonial dress wandering the lawn," she said.

"Really?" I said.

"We thought it might be one of our docents, but everyone was accounted for and the plantation was closed."

"Who saw her?" I said.

"I don't think I was here at the time," the docent said. "I don't know."

Disappointed, I stopped my interrogation. No matter; I already had another plan. At home, I emailed my ghost-hunting instructor. Yes. A year before, I'd joined a paranormal investigators group through Meetup.com. The leader offered a "Ghosthunting 101" course at Ben Lomond Plantation in Manassas, Virginia. No doubt this contributed to my strange confidence that I would sense Sarah at Scotchtown. I'd also attended investigations at other places: Point Lookout Lighthouse in southern Maryland; Old House Woods near Diggs, Virginia; and Bull Run Battlefield just down the road from my house. The more experienced members brought closed-circuit cameras, infrared thermometers, electromagnetic field detectors, and high-grade digital voice recorders. Next to filming an actual ghost, catching understandable words—an Electric Voice Phenomenon—on a recorder was a pinnacle of success for a paranormal investigation. The advanced investigators had audio editing software on their computers that could slow down and clear up recordings to more easily hear spectral voices. After each investigation we gathered to discuss our cumulative data. At Ben Lomond, I strapped my cassette recorder to my head. I recorded myself peeing, but not much else. My cheap digital camera sometimes caught white shining orbs. There was always debate over whether round white orbs caught on camera were spectral entities or dust. Except for me, the group was thorough, professional, and tough—investigations happened overnight, ideally in cold weather, when ghosts could, in theory, more easily gather the energy to materialize.

"It would be the perfect place for an investigation," I told the group leader Harris in my email. He contacted the APVA, explained that our nighttime investigation would be done with utmost respect for the property, and was refused. Perhaps the docents had experienced unprofessional ghosthunters. No matter; I was already forming a new plan.

I would pop into my local Fairfax County library for an hour to learn what life was like for Sarah, before and during her illness. I would learn what kind of husband and founding father shuts his mad wife up in the basement. I soon went over my one-hour estimate—several months over. It didn't feel like an obsession. My OCD had been different, painful in a way that my search for Sarah wasn't. The OCD had consisted of imaginary scenarios I knew not to be true, but which I kept worrying might be true. Not handwashing, but overthinking. "Did I bite the Band-Aid of that woman holding onto the bus bar? Did I bite her Band-Aid?" This could go on for hours. Or, "Did I take a can from the food aid box and put it in my backpack?" Then I'd open and close my bag several times to make sure I hadn't. My search for Sarah was not "obsessive," a word used too often and incorrectly in colloquial rhetoric. My search for Sarah stemmed more from sheer stubbornness.

Right away I discovered that Patrick's "Give me liberty" speech was not written down until 1817 by William Wirt, Patrick's first biographer and an author known to sacrifice fact for drama. For his opus *Sketches of The Life and Character of Patrick Henry*, Wirt's primary sources were Henry's friends and contemporaries, who probably had their own agendas. Wirt acknowledged the muddle of hand-me-down data; he noted in his appendix that his correspondents' "...statements were, in several instances, diametrically opposed to each other; and were, sometimes, all contradicted by the public prints, or the records of the state." Translation: Patrick's speech, which had been glorified in my U.S. history books since I was a child, had never happened.

As shocked as I was, I still believed that Sarah's story was true and discoverable. After all, an accurate account of Patrick's legacy was retained in reams of contemporary letters written by and about him, enough to sort out "what probably happened" with fair accuracy. Right? Wrong.

After Wirt had been writing his biography of Henry for a while, he called it "an irksome labor." When I read this, my disdain for Wirt faded somewhat, because I myself was increasingly irked by my own Sarah project gnawing and clawing at me. I spent days in libraries around Northern Virginia and the Washington D.C. area, including the Library of Congress, the Library of the Association for the Preservation of Virginia Antiquities (APVA), and the George Mason University library. Then I spent hours trying to remember which notes had come from which libraries. I collected different color folders from the stationery section at Giant, in hopes that I could build a picture of Sarah if only I put the correct data in the correct folder. At the grocery store, I was optimistic, but in the libraries, she refused to materialize from any archives. More from stubbornness than optimism, I continued to plumb the databases and card catalogs. I remained certain that she was in the file cabinets somewhere, dusty and sulking. Finally I dropped my head onto some library desk somewhere and admitted to myself that all I had was the Standard Sarah Story that had already been over-circulated by a random sampling of unreliable biographers, Internet pundits, local Hanover County historians, and even the *Washington Post*. And I had a bunch of paper cuts.

The Standard Sarah Story:

After the birth of her sixth child, Sarah developed "a strange antipathy" to her family and had to be put in the care of a Negro servant, or nursemaid, or other euphemism for slave, as well as "confined in the half-basement" with her arms crossed over her chest in a "strait-dress," because she was "deranged." The first two quotes are family lore, passed down for generations. The second two quotes come from a few vague lines, puffy with adjectives, written by the son of the doctor who treated Sarah.

The Standard Sarah Story only raised more questions for me. What constituted "deranged" to an eighteenth-century doctor? What constituted "antagonism"? Was she a lunatic, or a woman who spoke her mind? Even today, doctors are more likely to dismiss women's complaints than men's. Three centuries ago, I imagined, a woman who spoke loudly or asserted herself could easily be branded "crazy," just as today she could easily be branded "bitchy." I'd had my own experiences with dismissive doctors, mostly male.

The OCD hit me in my twenties, as a result of a then-undiagnosed Lyme Disease infection that combined physical pain and exhaustion with my mental issues. A psychiatrist fixed the OCD, but my body was a different story. Several primary care physicians, a neurologist, a sports medicine specialist, and a rheumatologist hadn't been able to unravel my symptoms. They prescribed several antidepressants, a sun lamp, St. John's Wort tea, and psychological counseling, and generally didn't suggest follow-up appointments. If I hadn't had rest, good nutrition, and strong family support, I might very well have died, either from suicide or the Lyme, if it got into my heart. I might have left my spirit floating around my bedroom, screaming and clutching its head. I had no proof that Sarah's soul did this; I just thought that was what I personally would do, if I were disembodied.

After years of intermittent burning veins and heavy limbs, I was used to fighting my way through life. Perhaps I wanted to see Sarah's fight, there in the basement. Tired though I was, I drove several hours to Richmond, to the Library of Virginia. On a city street, I heard screams behind me after I'd just changed lanes. In my rear view mirror, I saw a woman prostrate across two lanes. The road was busy, and a van had stopped near her. In the old OCD days, I would have worried I'd been the one to hit her. But that day, I knew it had been someone else. I hadn't felt a thump, hadn't seen anyone when I changed lanes, and the chaos seemed completely separate from my driving path. I didn't stop; many people already had. I felt horrible for the woman, but of necessity my mind moved to other things, like Sarah. Not until I was in my hotel room did I realize that I'd come from being a person whose heart jumped whenever my car hit a bump, thinking it might be a person, to someone who could logically see I hadn't been involved in a nearby accident. I fell backwards onto the bed, my clear head on the pillow and my ill, leaden limbs on the blanket.

At the Library of Virginia the archivist and I performed the thrilling ritual of putting on the white gloves before she allowed me to open boxes of Patrick Henry's papers. I'd found their reference numbers in a card catalog where even the cards were chilled from the extreme air-conditioning. I wore my coat and white gloves as I opened each box.

"Breathe," I reminded myself. "But not on the papers." I turned the pages of letters and ledgers in slow arcs. I was being careful, and I was also taking my time deciphering the curled and crossed 18th Century handwriting. I felt guilty at my irritation with the script. My own handwriting was so terrible that once in a work meeting, a coworker looked at my notebook and said, in all seriousness, "Oh, I didn't know you could write Arabic!" So I proceeded through the papers in as gentle and nonjudgmental manner as I could. In my impatience, I could easily miss the word "Sarah."

Then there it was. Buried in a musty box of Patrick's letters was an illegible number in a ledger entry, "Cloth for Sallie's clothes." My reams of reading had paid off. I knew that Sarah's nickname was Sallie. My heart beat faster as I realized how close I'd come to missing this. . . this. . . this. . . pretty much irrelevant information. Still, to me the moment was warm and magical. Between "Cloth for Sallie's clothes" and my logical, non-OCD response to the woman lying in the street, I considered this research trip rather auspicious. When I returned to my hotel room, the phone rang. A friend from the area wanted me to come out for a drink. First, I couldn't drink because one sip of alcohol made me feel woozy and achy almost immediately. Second, after hours in those cold archives, my adrenaline tank gauge was bumping on Empty. Everything I did, even my workweek, I fought through on adrenaline after a series of nap-infused days. I held my nose and told my friend I had a bad cold. It seemed easier. I had a fear of people thinking I was nutty for being sandbag heavy with exhaustion, after just reading for a few hours. Sarah's story reeked of such judgment, from her contemporaries to people nowadays. Perhaps that was another reason I wanted to be closer to her.

At Scotchtown I took a dozen pictures of Sarah's bedroom, but none showed an orb or any strange blurry bits that could be interpreted as, for example, a tormented face. I did not consider myself a gore-obsessed gawker. That described the other people visiting Scotchtown, hovering around her bedroom shivering and saying how "creeped out" they were. My sharper scorn I saved for the people who tried to capitalize on her drama, drama that may or may not have ever even happened—some guy who wrote a play about Sarah, the woman who wrote a children's novel with a stupid paragraph on the back about how maybe Patrick stole his "Give me liberty or give me death" speech from one of Sarah's basement wailings. I skimmed the play and novel and then dismissed them as pathos from the pens of people who had not ever been crazy themselves. Sarah and I, we had our little proprietary "been there" club. That much I knew.

To my exasperation, Patrick's biographers couldn't even agree if she was "dark" or "fair." Although she was descended from King Edward the First, and her father, John Shelton, owned thousands of acres in counties across Virginia, and Patrick's brother-in-law, Colonel Samuel Meredith, described her as "a woman of some fortune and much respectability," she only appears in the written record as a prop in the Story of Patrick. Among the reams of Henry records at Scotchtown, and all the libraries I visited, Sarah peeks in from the periphery: for example, in county deed books as "Patrick Henry, and Sarah his wife."

In the Fairfax Regional Library near my home, I bent over a small table in the empty Virginia Room. An oscillating fan rustled my notes and threatened to flutter away my finger-bookmarked pages. Distracted, I stood to stretch my cramping calves and wait for the head rush to dissipate. I'd seen these intense sparkle-spot movies ever since I began feeling tired and achy and burny, but the doctors paid no attention when I mentioned them. I felt only half-seen. Half-seen, in the 21st Century. As I wandered through the stacks and past the librarian's desk, I assessed my leg energy levels and wondered if I should go home.

"Can I help you?" said a woman behind the desk. I jumped. My body also had an extreme startle response. Once when someone popped a champagne cork at a party, I fell down. Here I steadied myself against the desk. I explained my project, and how I feared I'd fallen in love with an impossible task. The librarian didn't bullshit me.

"Yes, it's going to be tough," she said. "Women had no rights, so we left no paper trail." As she spoke, I felt sadder and madder on Sarah's behalf. The librarian continued, looking rather pissed off herself, "Women were behind the scenes until their husbands died, and they got something, like rich." I liked the sarcastic word-play in her speech and after a quick thanks rushed back to my table to write it down. Poor Sarah made the mistake of dying before Patrick.

My interaction with the Virginia Room librarian convinced me that if I were going to write about Sarah, I would have to research her world and then put a lot of "perhaps" and "I imagine" and "could have" language in the text. There was less information about daily life for privileged east-coast families in the 18th Century than there was for such 19th Century people, but I found enough. Pertinent to Sarah, I noted the lack of birth control, how women's young married years comprised a constant train of pregnancies, and how while the lower-class and foreigners often gave birth by squatting, the upper classes and even many poorer Americans were adopting bed births. Squatting was supposed to be healthier. Sarah, probably through no choice of her own, used a bed. The Standard Sarah Story says she derailed after the birth of her sixth child, Eddie. Because her illness, according to oral history, happened not long after Eddie's birth, some of Sarah's contemporaries assumed that she went mad from the pressures of raising six children. I felt this assumption was sexist. I had no kids, but I'd gone crazy anyway. Moreover, in Sarah's day many women had far more than six children, and lived to tell about it. In Sarah's day, society prized fecund women, who could provide extra people to make money or carry down a family legacy. I assessed that any contemporary mutterings about how Sarah went crazy after Eddie's birth were probably tinged with scorn: "...And after only six children!"

I couldn't have children, because I didn't have the energy to raise them. As a toddler, I'd seen my mother sicken to a 106-degree fever after a bug bite, and I saw her never regain her passion for camping or her former award-winning tennis playing. When I broke up with a much-loved boyfriend because he wanted a child, I told myself that I chose not to have children, but maybe I was simply following the commands of my body. In either case, I was lucky to live in 21st Century U.S.A., where no one judged me for not breeding enough. Oh. Except for my friends' friend, a near stranger to me, who said, "You'll want kids once you meet the right person," days after I'd broken up with the right person because I didn't want, or couldn't raise, a child. And except for the colleague who asked me if I had children.

"No," I said.

"You mean, not yet," she said. She smiled.

And then there was the neighbor who approached me as I carried out the garbage. That afternoon, a mass of children of all ages skated and ran and skipped and biked in our cul-de-sac with precious few adults looking on. My neighbor said they were her children and grandchildren, and wasn't it wonderful? She smiled and tilted her head.

"Do you have children?" she said.

"No," I said.

"Oh," her mouth said, but her face, lips, and weeble-wobble head said, "How sad for you, all alone in that townhouse."

I played these scenes over and over in my head, whenever I read about Sarah's supposed Death by Childrearing. Were our 21st Century attitudes toward women's reproduction much different from those in the U.S. colonial days? Yes, of course, but also not.

Sarah may have died from the physicality of Eddie's birth, not from the exhaustion of raising six children. Some historians wonder if Sarah may have developed an infection during or after the birth. As my Lyme infection contributed to my OCD, Sarah's presumed infection could have led to post-partum psychosis, an extreme version of postpartum depression. Modern medicine describes some of the symptoms as: delusions, insomnia, anxiety, suicidal or homicidal inclinations, guilt, fatigue, confusion, mood swings, and—understandably—irritability. Did Sarah show some or all of these symptoms? Did she unleash them on Patrick and her children? What about the slave or slaves forced to care for her? (Although I'd been naively startled at the lack of documentation of Sarah's misadventures, I was not surprised that I found no source, primary or otherwise, that mentioned how the enslaved servants felt about this supposed mad woman in the basement. History had reduced them to props in Sarah's already meager story.)

At a local Ashland library, someone on staff probably noticed the shadows and pink rims around my eyes, which came both from reading 18th Century handwriting and also were part of my daily existence with the un-diagnosed Lyme disease. She probably felt sorry for me, or for Sarah, because she gave me the names and numbers of some still-living descendants of the Henrys, as well as some other long-lived locals who might reveal something new about Sarah's insanity. Back home in Centreville, I sat at my kitchen table and made the calls. Everyone I spoke to had the grind of age in their voice. After driving to and from Ashland, I desperately wanted to lie down, but I needed to sound and feel professional, and that required sitting. I tried not to feel self-pity when my body started to hurt, because the days when I'd had both body pain and OCD were not long gone. Nonetheless, halfway through the interviews I stretched across the table and rested my head on my arm. Everyone was happy to talk about Sarah. They were happy to talk, period. Their tales veered across centuries and family ties until my notes looked like a Jackson Pollack composition of spiked and curled text connected (sort of) by arrows, with many scribble-overs as the interviewees corrected themselves. Their accounts were remarkably consistent for a two-hundred-year-old legend. To summarize from my Pollacked notes: For the last three years of her life, Sarah was insane and lived confined in one (or maybe two) rooms of the basement with a black housemaid or nurse, (no doubt a slave). Patrick went down—or passed food—through a trapdoor in the hall to feed his crazy wife in the strait-dress. Sarah either didn't see her children, or she only saw them when she had infrequent spells of normality.

Other local folklore and family tradition passed down in print by numerous Patrick biographers follows a similar plot. Sarah spent her last three years in the basement of Scotchtown feeling despondent, "helpless, unable to care for herself, and subject to fits of lunacy," in danger of "destroying herself or harming those around her," and "off in some far-away fantasy world." The more than thirty years she spent as a healthy homemaker are largely forgotten, in favor of her ostensibly dramatic end.

Ultimately I found only three primary sources documenting Sarah's sickness, and none of them mentioned the basement. The son of Sarah's physician, Dr. Thomas Hinde, called Sarah "deranged" and wrote about his father's experience of treating her, somewhat after the fact:

> [Patrick Henry's] soul was bowed down and bleeding under the heaviest sorrows and personal distress. His beloved companion had lost her reason, and could only be restrained from self-destruction by a strait-dress. I cannot reflect on my venerable deceased father's rehearsal of the particulars, without feeling myself almost a bleeding heart. It was such men that Almighty God raised up to assert and maintain our rights.

This was powerful stuff. Wouldn't someone, anyone, who had lived it, feel compelled to write it down in their journal, or in a letter to a trusted friend? Nope. In October 1774, four months before Sarah died, Patrick's sister Anne wrote in a letter to a family friend, "My brother Pat is not returned from Philadelphia, yet his wife is extremely ill." That's it. Denied. Anne said the details were "too much to write," and with that simple line she frustrated and infuriated historians ever since, especially me. I wanted the details, no matter how gritty. I still considered myself more noble than the midnight seancers, but to be honest, what would I have done if I'd found a letter telling how the strait-dress blistered her arms (as it might have, had it existed) and what words she screamed as she threw herself against the earthen walls (if she did so), and how she felt when Dr. Hinde disrobed her modestly (if it happened that way) in order to bleed her, and where did he bleed her from? Using what tools? If I'd found such a letter, how would I have used it in my research project, the essay written for my professor? Would my own account be as superficial and lurid as all the others?

Maybe, by asking these concrete questions, I was trying to compensate for my lack of knowledge about my own illness. Even when my doctor and I figured out I had Lyme disease, I felt no fireworks of hope, but rather the yellow specks peppering the mouth of a dying Pacman: dubadubadubadubadooooo… Sigh. No one knew how to treat Lyme disease, and worse, medical and scientific and political professionals argued about how to treat it, in endless dodge-ball rhetoric where the patients were the net. Old-school big medicine (The Infectious Diseases Society of America, The National Institutes of Health, Yale University, Johns Hopkins University, The Mayo Clinic, and The Centers for Disease Control) believed that the physiologically tricky Lyme bacteria, which is the only organism on the planet that uses manganese instead of iron to metabolize oxygen, among other talents, could undoubtedly be killed by several weeks of an antibiotic such as doxycycline. Any persisting symptoms, they said, were the patient's imagination, or a "post-Lyme" immune response. They wouldn't consider that the bacteria might still be alive. Clinicians who actually saw Lyme patients in their offices thought differently. They treated with long-term or pulsed antibiotic regimens, and sometimes lost their licenses for it. They and their patients went broke paying for court fees and medicine respectively, until they disappeared like the dying Pacman.

Sarah experienced a similar crash of the treatment titans. A new appreciation of science and education was filtering through the upper classes, and almost certainly Sarah's doctor and her husband would have considered her condition medical, even if they didn't know the cause. The old ways still prevailed, though. The Scotchtown docent said many of Sarah's contemporaries believed she was demon-possessed. I felt sure I knew the look they would have given her. I'd received stares and glares from numerous doctors who thought there was something wrong with my mental state and why was I wasting their time in a medical office? Upstairs in Scotchtown, a portrait of Sarah's deep-browed uncle, Joseph Shelton, glared, stared, and seemed to watch me skitter across the sitting room. I decided that he, and not Sarah and I, was likely the possessed one.

I was ready to call off the search when I had a major research success. I found tantalizing and almost contemporary mentions of Sarah's life in a memoir written by Patrick's sister Elizabeth. Several of Patrick's reputable biographers cited this book, including two who actually quoted from it directly, including quotation marks.

Elizabeth's book *Paths of Glory* appeared to be the original source for most of the Established Sarah Facts, such as that Patrick bought Scotchtown to aid in her health, that her illness made Henry "distraught," that none of her doctors "could quiet her mental disturbance," and that Patrick's friends told him to send Sarah to the mental institution but his family disagreed, and that she was "confined to one of the airy, sunlit rooms in the half-basement" two or three years before Christmas 1774, because she had developed an "antipathy" to her husband and children.

Later historians believed she also had to share the house with Patrick's relatives, the Paynes, another couple with multiple children. I suspected that if she in fact went nuts, those extra visitors would have been what cracked her. When my boyfriend—not the one who wanted a child—moved his own children into my house, I developed a "strange antipathy" toward my boyfriend and his eighteen-year-old daughter and ten-year-old son. I was ill; they were noisy and messy. I moved a mattress into a small bedroom, put all my light-blue bedding and light-blue-themed artwork on the walls and called it my "padded room." Here I retreated when the "strange antipathy" threatened to burst from my lungs.

Somehow—shock blurred my memory of the moment—I discovered that *Paths of Glory* was not actually written by Patrick's sister Elizabeth, but was a historical novel written by Nelly C. Preston, Elizabeth's great-great-granddaughter. By digging into citations upon citations as if making my project's own grave, I learned that Preston had assembled *Paths of Glory* from undocumented family stories. Then Patrick's 1957 biographer Robert Douthat Meade interviewed her as one of his prime sources, then spun much of what she said as nonfiction, which he peppered with quotation marks. Other biographers quoted Meade's quotes from *Paths of Glory*, and a historical novel became local legend became part of the docent spiel at Scotchtown.

"AAAAARRRRGGGGHHHH!" echoed through my brain for hours after I made this connection.

The APVA keeps Scotchtown manor as it probably was during Patrick's lifetime. If Sarah did live in the basement, her room was small, with just enough room for a chest, a night stand, a cupboard, and a narrow bed with a straw mattress. She would have watched the world at lawn level from the basement half-windows. The panes were about twice the height of Sarah's face, set deeply into the thick walls, providing a broad sill she could have clung to when her arms were not restrained. The windows revealed a view of grass, clipped short sometimes by slaves with scythes, but more often tended by sheep who were allowed to roam and snack at will. Most versions of the legend say that after she sickened, Sarah didn't see her children. I imagined perhaps she watched their legs when they played on the lawn or ran between outbuildings.

Another bombshell hit my research-rattled brain. On one of my later tours of Scotchtown, the docent said that, because of its fireplace and the natural insulation of the soil under the flag-rock floor, Sarah's basement bedroom ("If she really did stay in the basement," I thought) was the warmest room in the house in winter and the coolest room in summer. Oh. Well, that did take away some of the drama, didn't it? But it didn't change the fact that she was locked up (if she was). I turned in the room and pondered as the tour continued without me. Underneath her straw mattress, ropes hung across the bed frame to support the mattress. The phrase "sleep tight" comes from the then-regular habit of pulling and re-knotting the ropes to make the mattress lie firmer. Presumably a slave did this for Sarah. I hoped she (not to mention the slave, who may have been dodging hurled bedpans for all I knew) did sleep tight. I almost never slept well, due to my brain inflammation and general metabolic mayhem. At least I wasn't locked up. But then maybe I was—locked away from life, anyway, trapped in a body that looked "normal" and intact, but which couldn't run, couldn't catch its breath, had tinnitus in one or both ears (depending on the day and the alignment of Mars and Pluto), and hurt like a bruise when it bumped into anything, which it did a lot, especially my co-worker's cubicle walls. As I continued to survey her room, I once again chastised myself not to complain. If I was trapped in an icky-feeling body, at least I was no longer trapped in a tormented mind. There was a time I might have benefited from a strait-jacket myself, for example, when my college boyfriend asked me what I wanted for lunch right while I was trying to reason away an OCD worry. It might have been, "Did I bump the pile of watermelons and crush the little girl? No, because I was too far away. Too far away. Too far away." I had to count "far away" on five fingers, but my boyfriend interrupted me on three. I spurted tears from my eyes and spit from my sobbing mouth before I knocked the light switch out of the wall. By instinct, my boyfriend grabbed my upper arms and restrained me against the bed.

If Sarah were restrained, her bindings were probably more humane than the shackles at the new "Public Hospital For Persons of Insane and Disordered Minds" in Williamsburg. Later known as Eastern State Asylum, this facility housed the mad and the misunderstood. They lived in small, dirty cells with barred windows. Wardens removed the chains during medical treatments, which included cold-water dunking chairs and blistering ointments.

In contrast, Patrick and the Scotchtown staff treated Sarah as a princess. Patrick put Sarah under the care of Dr. Hinde, his personal physician. His cures, though similar to the techniques used in the Williamsburg asylum, were probably not administered as often or as brutally. Judging from the healing techniques of the day, Dr. Hinde likely treated Sarah with the colonial cure-all phlebotomy, or bloodletting. He may have also tried administering opium, a painkiller still used in different forms today.

My psychiatrist, Dr. Stein, was far less ethical than Dr. Hinde. In fact, *The Washington Post* revealed him to be quite mad. I should have noticed something awry when he encouraged me to go up and up and up on my Luvox, even though I'd told him I felt "mostly better."

"Why settle for mostly, when you could be completely better?" He was a big man with white lionish hair. He roared.

He'd obviously never had OCD. In OCD "mostly" is nigh on heaven. No one ever really gets to "completely." I stopped at the FDA's 300 milligram maximum because I didn't trust doctors anymore. For the same reason, I started weaning myself down, very slowly. In the meantime, I called to make a follow-up with Dr. Stein, and the receptionist told me his license had been taken away. *The Post* headline read: "Virginia Doctor's Misconduct Left Trail of Broken Lives. Medical System Failed to Protect Patients." The front-page article said that Dr. Stein flew with one patient to her childhood home in Illinois to encourage the woman to remember childhood abuses—for instance, that her father had been in a satanic cult and had forced her to kill and eat a baby. According to the article, a "22-page [court] order details ethical breaches, misdiagnoses and the inappropriate and excessive prescribing of drugs, including narcotics, in the treatment of 10 patients Stein saw between 1991 and 2000." The authors cited a "report based on more than 100 interviews with former patients and their families, physicians, hospital officials…"

As I read, fear and fury swirled together in my reddening cheeks. Could I have died like one of his patients did, whose death certificate he ostensibly signed in a way to steer attention away from the medicine-induced toxins in the patient's system? Would he have eventually bound my ankles in duct tape, as he did to a four-year-old patient, according to the *Post*? Would I have been so desperate to keep the OCD at bay that I might have submitted to these injustices? I could not say no.

I took two years to wean off the 300 mg daily dose of Luvox. That whole time, I did not see a doctor. Matters were in my own, duct-tape-free hands. Sarah certainly didn't have the empowerment and self-authority that would have allowed her to dictate the extent or nature of Hinde's treatments, none of which were documented in primary sources. For all I knew, he might have signed a sketchy death certificate or two.

Brave biographer Meade—earning his rank as the Patrick Henry researcher most cited by subsequent writers—combed innumerable land deeds to determine that "[Sarah's] condition was pitiful" in her last couple years because her signature did not appear on most of the Henrys' land sale transactions, except for the last one, on August 22, 1774. Meade concluded that she either "had a lucid interval, or the local farmers tactfully overlooked her mental condition." Or maybe she wasn't a lunatic after all. I saw many deeds and paperwork where Sarah's signature didn't show up. Meade may have been really stretching to find her. I knew the feeling.

In the years after biographers Wirt and Meade, a series of eager Patrick biographers plumbed local Henry descendants for details on his life and, incidentally, that of his wife. Whenever I felt vexed, I imagined the biographers panicking as time went on, and direct descendants became fewer. In their hysteria, the biographers quoted loose-lipped locals, and the biographers quoted each other, and somewhere in the mess began the "strait-dress" phenomenon: all over the Patrick Henry literature, from much-cited biographer Meade's 1957 biography to *The Washington Post*, Sarah's "strait-dress" appeared in quotation marks, which give it a cache and ethos as if it were a fully-documented fact. It wasn't. The Sarah-keyword "strait-dress"—in fact, the very existence of Sarah's restraining device—appears in plenty of books and articles, but in no primary sources.

Some tourists, articles, or biographers hypothesized that Sarah sickened because cold, uncaring Patrick left her alone so often as he gallivanted across the eastern seaboard of Virginia on political business. This irritated me, because my father was very often away on business, and he was not cold and uncaring, and my mother didn't collapse into lunacy. She kept our houses and my sister and me in top-notch condition, except for that time I bit my sister's nose and she needed stitches.

Patrick was likely stricken by Sarah's illness, assessed Colonial Williamsburg Foundation researcher and interpreter Mark Couvillon. He sought solace at church during Sarah's decline.

Most accounts put Sarah's death in early 1775, when she was thirty-seven. No one knows how she died. Infection? Anorexia? Suicide?

My last of the three golden contemporary-source nuggets came from Patrick's friend Philip Mazzei, who said Patrick confided to him that Sarah's death had "forced [Patrick] to abandon all things which recalled her to him." To me, Patrick seemed rather successful in this. Two years after Sarah died, he married Dorothea Dandridge, a woman in Patrick's social circle, two decades younger than he was. Today, no one even knows where Sarah is buried.

The lack of a headstone might have meant that Sarah's family was ashamed or superstitious about her "distraction." Or it might not. Only one in ten graves in colonial Virginia were marked, regardless of the sanity of the person therein. However, often those graves did not need stones, because they were in family cemeteries where survivors knew the locations of their loved ones' bodies. According to docents, Scotchtown does not have a Henry family cemetery, hence the idea that Sarah's family kept her resting site secret as tradition demanded for the demon-possessed. But educated people like Patrick and Dr. Hinde understood that mental illness could have physical causes, so perhaps Patrick took his wife to Mt. Brilliant to be buried in the family cemetery with his father. But yet—transport and embalming difficulties would have made it more practical to put Sarah to rest under the ground of her last home.

So where is she?

On the grounds of Scotchtown grows a wide-ranging patch of periwinkle, a preferred ground covering for graves in colonial America. Periwinkle does not grow wild. According to docents at Scotchtown, the APVA has the technology to find out what's under the periwinkle. But they don't want to know. They fear this knowledge will encourage tomb robbers. Maybe all of us—me, the biographers, Nelly C. Preston, the mouthy locals, the thieves—wanted something a little more than "She married, she kept it all together, she lost it, she died."

As the periwinkle brushed my ankles, I remembered the periwinkle surrounding my grandparents' house in Michigan, the only "permanent" home I'd ever known, as a child growing up with a father in the U.S. State Department. We moved from house to house, from country to country. I was told to savor all the new experiences, but I didn't. I disliked packing up my bedroom but eventually grew good at it. My mom packed up the whole rest of each house. The periwinkle tickled my ankle, and the gears in my brain ground still for a moment, like the end of an exhale. They then rotated in a new direction. I had pages of notes about Sarah when she was a healthy mother of five. I'd largely ignored them in favor of the legend of her death. New thoughts occurred to me there in the periwinkle: At her most hectic, Sarah was riding in wagons with five kids, probably several trunks, maybe some slaves who might have driven the wagons, and possibly some favored pets or livestock, across the rumpled Virginia country roads. At least my mom had "sea freight" and "air freight" and only two little girls, both darling angels who would never even consider stealing the glass jars of strawberry and blueberry jelly from the business class food trays. Because I wanted to see how Sarah's peripatetic existence compared to mine, I patched together my notes about her pre-basement life. This took many hours, in several sessions at the kitchen table. Occasionally I went back to the microfiches and flicked through the musty books, at least one of which was the kind that you had to cut the pages yourself before reading. I actually had to cut a couple in the index. Toward the end, as a picture came into view, I had to move my notes to the living room floor.

Sarah and Patrick started out financially strapped but in love. According to Meade, "The marriage was a turning point in his career."

Sarah brought to the marriage 300 acres of sandy soil called Piny Slash—or Pine Slash, or Pine Slashes, or Piney Slash—perhaps named for the second-growth scrub pine that had reclaimed the land after a previous farmer. Sarah came to Patrick with a dowry of the land, money, and six young slaves—an icky present, but one related matter-of-factly by biographers. Hence his marriage to Sarah provided him a critical stepping-stone in his quest for self-sufficiency.

But the beginning was tough. Piny Slash was not a fecund farm. In the short, parched summer of 1755, when she was seventeen, Sarah gave birth to Martha. Baby Johnny arrived in 1757. But by then John Shelton couldn't stand to see his daughter and grandchildren struggle through another harvest at Piny Slash. He invited Patrick to manage the Sheltons' profitable tavern across from the Hanover Courthouse, and Patrick took an interest in law.

The family moved often, as Patrick's public service career dictated. Every couple years Sarah shuttled her children in wagons across the lumpy Virginia countryside. With each move, there were a few more trunks to be stacked and at least one more child to be lifted into the carriage.

William was born in 1763. Baby Annie came in 1767. Two years later Sarah added a fifth child, Elizabeth, to the growing brood. Patrick's political passions took him away for weeks or months, while Sarah remained behind, overseeing "staff," house matters, supplies, and children. Their estates varied from extremely basic in the beginning to comfortably lavish at Sarah's end.

Scotchtown plantation was the Henrys' last home together. Sarah did not have a chance to enjoy its opulence. Her health did not flourish in a family with two toddlers and two teenagers who, according to Colonel Meredith, were "wild as young colts." Her oldest daughter, Martha, helped her manage the plantation while Patrick thundered across the countryside on horseback to courts or political assemblies. In 1771, came Edward. And Sarah sickened.

The bug bite that floored my own mother happened in India, when I was about three, and my little sister about one. Our mom was medivac-level-sick, and she never really recovered completely. Granted, a twentieth-century medivac from India to the U.S. and back is better than a one-way ticket to an eighteenth-century colonial basement. I could, however, imagine Martha, William, John, Annie, Elizabeth, and Edward not having their mother accessible and growing closer to their other relatives, the way I grew closer to my aya, whom I came to regard as a co-mother. In my earliest memory, a dream, I'm trapped in my mosquito net. When I scream for help, both my mom and Divi open the door to my bedroom.

Before my sister and I went to college, my mom almost single-handedly moved us and our dad either across town or across the world no less than fifteen times. My dad's job was to blame, or to thank, depending on my mood. He was often away, traveling on business, working long hours, and taking on projects for which he received much acclaim, but the only reason he could do all that was because my mom was there behind the scenes, taking care of family, home, and life logistics.

She did all this while still tired achy from her bug encounter years before. Sarah performed the same feats of family organization, with more children but apparently good health, until Scotchtown. It all evens out in the end. I would carry my own bug-instigated illness for fifteen years before diagnosis, then for several years more until antibiotic treatment began to work. I remained in the same house for thirteen years, too weak to change homes and not beholden to a husband. I felt stuck. Perhaps that was yet another circumstance that drew me to Sarah, including the dead, sick, and live versions of her. As I pieced together the story of Sarah's moves and remembered bits of my family's moves, I realized that although I'd been feeling stuck ever since the illness struck when I was twenty-one, I'd already lived quite a lot.

Speaking of having lived a lot, had I lived in Scotchtown in the 1770s? Of course not. Even I, a budding paranormal investigator and fan of reincarnation theories, understood that no one who claims to be the reincarnation of a famous person, such as Sarah has become, was actually the reincarnation of that person. A more probable reincarnation of Sarah Henry was likely to be some male advertising executive in Nashville or Los Angeles, for example.

I did shiver a bit when my classmate Lisa, after she read a short draft I'd written about Sarah, said, "You know, Christina, when I was reading, the whole time I was imagining that Sarah looked like you. I kept picturing you in that basement room. I kept seeing you in that strait-dress. You wrote that she had dark hair and dark eyes. You have dark hair and dark eyes." She'd missed the part where I moaned that historians were conflicted about even her hair color. A small desktop portrait in Scotchtown, painted long after her death by an artist who never saw her, did show her looking a bit like me, I supposed. Dark hair, dark eyes, a little paunch to her cheeks. Did the artist put a haunted look in her eyes and a tint of circles beneath them? I saw those in the mirror every time I had a "bad body day." I saw them on my mom's face during long airplane rides to distant places.

Patrick sold Scotchtown to one Wilson Miles Cary. In April 1782, Cary put an ad in *The Virginia Gazette* for the estate's sale: "The crops of wheat from this land are equal to any I am acquainted with. There are eight rooms upon the first floor, with most delightful cellars under them. . ."

I returned to Fairfax Regional just in case I'd missed something. Behold, I did find a Patrick biography that I hadn't read before. The index listed an entry for "Henry, Sarah Shelton—see Shelton, Sarah." I flipped to the S's, just as manically as I had in dozens of other books over the last many months. Flip flip. The last page of the book—the page with Shelton, Sarah—was missing.

Today, you can get married at Scotchtown. According to the APVA website, Scotchtown's "deep history and classic views recall the intimate splendor of a rich, romantic past." Parents receive free admission on Mothers' and Fathers' Days, along with a complimentary ice cream. I imagine Sarah rolling over in her grave. Wherever it is.

Sources

Campbell, Norine Dickson. *Patrick Henry: Patriot and Statesman.* New York: Devin-Adair Publishers, 1969.

Couvillon, Mark. *Patrick Henry's Virginia.* Brookneal, Virginia: Patrick Henry Memorial Foundation, 2001.

Mayer, Henry. *A Son of Thunder: Patrick Henry and the American Republic.* New York/Toronto: Franklin Watts, 1986.

Mazzei, Philip. *Memoirs of the Life and Peregrinations of the Florentine Philip Mazzei 1730 - 1816.* Trans. Howard R. Marraro. New York: Columbia University Press, 1942.

Meade, Robert Douthat. *Patrick Henry, Patriot in the Making.* Philadelphia and New York: J.B. Lippincott Company, 1957.

Meade, Robert Douthat. *Patrick Henry, Practical Revolutionary.* Philadelphia and New York: J.B. Lippincott Company, 1969.

Morgan, George. *The True Patrick Henry.* Philadelphia: Lippincott 1907.

Patrick Henry Ledger and Account Book 1770-1774, Library of Virginia.

Preston, Nelly C. *Paths of Glory; A simple tale of a far-faring bride Elizabeth, sister of Patrick Henry.* Richmond, Virginia: Whittet and Shepperson, 1961.

Whitaker, Mrs. A.E. "The Shelton Family." St. Louis, Missouri, in *William and Mary College Quarterly Historical Magazine*, Second Series Jul. 1929.

Willison, George. *Patrick Henry and His World.* New York: Doubleday, 1969.

Wirt, William. *Sketches of the Life and Character of Patrick Henry.* 1841. Freeport, New York: Libraries Press, 1970.

Acknowledgements

I would like to thank all the docents at Scotchtown, DC and Virginia area librarians, Ashburn locals, and other historically informed people who took time to discuss with me the story of Sarah Henry and point me in the direction of helpful resources.

I appreciate the work of the late Robert Meade, the ultimate Henry biographer, whose research led me to primary sources and helped sort myth from fact. He struggled to put Patrick on the page just as much as I struggled to find Sarah.

Mary Kay Zuravleff, while a writing professor at George Mason University, guided me through the first draft of a nonfiction article on Sarah Henry. She met me multiple times outside of class hours to help me articulate the story of a woman who didn't have a story. With her help, that article became tight and polished. It was a crucial starting point for this personal essay, "And Sarah His Wife." Thank you from my heart, Mary Kay.

Most of all, I want to thank my parents Helen and Dave, my sister Caroline, and my partner Ben for their unwavering love, support, and encouragement.

About the Author

CHRISTINA DIANE CAMPBELL earned a MFA in Creative Non-fiction from George Mason University. She is the co-founder of *Onely.org*, where she writes about marital status discrimination, a topic she has also written on for *Atlantic.com*, *PsychologyToday.com*, and *Change.org*. Christina lives in Virginia, but fantasizes about settling someday in Leelanau County, MI with her cats.

This Year's Judge

Michigan Writers Cooperative Press would like to express our thanks to Neal Rubin for judging the Nonfiction manuscripts this year. We are grateful for his commitment of time, and for his commitment to helping Michigan Writers Cooperative Press develop and publish new voices.

NEAL RUBIN began writing his *Detroit News* column in June of 2000. His frequently light-hearted look at life appears Monday, Tuesday and Thursday in print and at www.detroitnews.com.

Rubin came to the *News* after 16 years as a feature writer and columnist with the *Detroit Free Press*, where his greatest achievement was getting banned by the World Wrestling Federation. In addition to his column, he writes the nationally syndicated comic strip "Gil Thorp," about a high school coach and the ever-changing cast of kids at Milford High School.

His last stop before Detroit was Las Vegas, where he was a three-time state sportswriter of the year in an admittedly limited field. A Michigander since 1984, Rubin grew up in Southern California and Colorado and attended the University of Northern Colorado on a 7-card stud scholarship. He prefers dogs to cats, game shows to reality shows, and writing to actual work.

This book was published in the spring of 2017 in a signed edition of 100 copies. Book design is by Heather Lee Shaw.

This chapbook is part of the Cooperative Series of the Michigan Writers Small Press Project, which was launched in 2005 to give members of Michigan Writers, Inc., a new avenue to publication. Authors share the publishing costs and marketing responsibilities with Michigan Writers in return for the prestige of being published by a press that prints only carefully selected manuscripts.

Manuscripts of poetry, short stories and essays are solicited from members and adjudicated by a panel of experienced writers once every year. For more information, please visit www.michwriters.org.

Michigan Writers is an open-membership organization dedicated to providing opportunities for networking, professional growth and publication for writers of all ages and skill levels in Northwest Lower Michigan.

OTHER TITLES AVAILABLE FROM
MICHIGAN WRITERS COOPERATIVE PRESS

Made in the USA
San Bernardino, CA
04 November 2018